SNOOPY

features as

The Great Entertainer

Charles M. Schulz

Originally published in 1990 as
'Snoopy Stars as the Entertainer'.
This edition published in 2002 by Ravette Publishing.

Printed and bound in Great Britain
for Ravette Publishing Limited,
Unit 3, Tristar Centre,
Star Road, Partridge Green,
West Sussex RH13 8RA
by Cox & Wyman, Berkshire.

ISBN: 1 84161 160 3

PEANUTS

They had named their Great Dane "Good Authority."

12-10

One day, she asked her husband if he had seen her new belt.

"Belt?" he said. "Oh, I'm sorry. I thought it was a dog collar. I have it on Good Authority."

Shortly thereafter, their marriage began to go downhill.

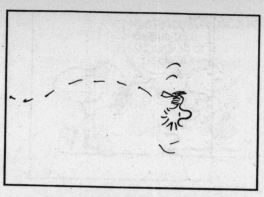

3-17

PAWPET
SHOW
1:00 P.M.

HOW DO YOU LIKE THE SHOW SO FAR?

IT'S PRETTY GOOD, I GUESS..

4-28

THEN SHE HEARD SOMEONE TALKING..

AND WHEN ALICE LOOKED UP, THERE WAS THE CHESHIRE CAT!

YOU'VE NEVER SEEN ME DO MY CHESHIRE BEAGLE TRICK, HAVE YOU?

YOU WANT TO SEE MY CHESHIRE BEAGLE TRICK AGAIN?

1-16

OKAY, HERE WE GO...

I'VE NEVER BEEN SO EMBARRASSED IN ALL MY LIFE..

TRY HOLDING YOUR BREATH..

WHAT'S GOING ON HERE?

WE'RE HAVING A LITTLE "RE-ENTRY" PROBLEM!

7-11

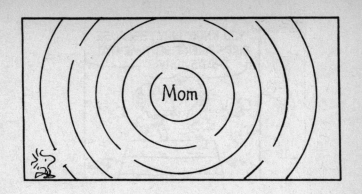

THIS IS MOTHER'S DAY, AND YOU'RE STILL LOOKING FOR YOUR MOM, HUH?

WELL, LITTLE FRIEND, I HATE TO TELL YOU THIS, BUT YOU'RE NEVER GOING TO FIND HER

5-13

10-13

Joe Murmur and his brothers were pickpockets.

10-15

They worked all the county fairs.

© 1977 United Feature Syndicate, Inc.

How did people know their pockets were being picked?

When a Murmur ran through the crowd.

A Short Story

by Snoopy

Everything he did began to annoy her.

8-1

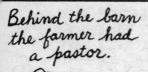

DO YOU LIKE BIRD STORIES? HERE'S A BIRD STORY...

THERE WAS THIS LITTLE BIRD, SEE, AND HE HAD BEEN VERY BAD..HIS MOTHER HAD YELLED AT HIM, AND HE FELT AWFUL...

© 1987 United Feature Syndicate, Inc.

10-23

DON'T MOVE, SIR! THE TEACHER IS EXPLAINING SOMETHING...

I'LL GET YOU FOR THIS, MARCIE!

3-14

I HAVE TO LEAVE NOW, SIR... I'M DELIVERING SOME MESSAGES FOR THE TEACHER...

I'LL GET YOU GOOD, MARCIE!

6-12

NEXT 2
MILES

2-26

© 1986 United Feature Syndicate,Inc.

SCHULZ

Other PEANUTS titles published by Ravette ...

Pocket Books	ISBN	Price
Man's Best Friend	1 84161 066 6	£2.99
Master of Disguise	1 84161 161 1	£2.99
Master of the Fairways	1 84161 067 4	£2.99
The Fearless Leader	1 84161 104 2	£2.99
The Fitness Fanatic	1 84161 029 1	£2.99
The Flying Ace	1 84161 027 5	£2.99
The Great Philosopher	1 84161 064 X	£2.99
The Legal Beagle	1 84161 065 8	£2.99
The Literary Ace	1 84161 026 7	£2.99
The Master Chef	1 84161 107 7	£2.99
The Matchmaker	1 84161 028 3	£2.99
The Music Lover	1 84161 106 9	£2.99
The Sportsman	1 84161 105 0	£2.99
The Tennis Ace	1 84161 162 X	£2.99
The Winter Wonder Dog	1 84161 163 8	£2.99

Little Books		
Charlie Brown - Friendship	1 84161 156 5	£2.50
Charlie Brown - Wisdom	1 84161 099 2	£2.50
Educating Peanuts	1 84161 158 1	£2.50
Lucy - Advice	1 84161 101 8	£2.50
Peanuts - Life	1 84161 157 3	£2.50
Peppermint Patty - Blunders	1 84161 102 6	£2.50
Snoopy - Laughter	1 84161 100 X	£2.50
Snoopy - Style	1 84161 155 7	£2.50

Colour Landscapes		
Passion for Peanuts	1 84161 153 0	£4.50
Snoopy Unleashed	1 84161 154 9	£4.50

Miscellaneous		
Peanuts Anniversary Treasury	1 84161 021 6	£9.99
Peanuts Treasury	1 84161 043 7	£9.99
You Really Don't Look 50 Charlie Brown	1 84161 020 8	£7.99

Snoopy's Laughter and Learning	ISBN	Price
Book 1 - Read with Snoopy	1 84161 016 X	£2.50
Book 2 - Write with Snoopy	1 84161 017 8	£2.50
Book 3 - Count with Snoopy	1 84161 018 6	£2.50
Book 4 - Colour with Snoopy	1 84161 019 4	£2.50

All PEANUTS books are available at your local bookshop or from the publisher at the address below. Just tick the titles required and send the form with your payment to:-

RAVETTE PUBLISHING, Unit 3, Tristar Centre, Star Road, Partridge Green, West Sussex RH13 8RA

Prices and availability are subject to change without prior notice.

Please enclose a cheque or postal order made payable to **Ravette Publishing** to the value of the cover price of the book and allow the following for UK postage and packing:-

55p for the first book + 30p for each additional book, except *You Really Don't Look 50 Charlie Brown* when please add £1.50 p&p per copy and the two *Treasuries* when please add £2.50 p&p per book.

Name ....

Address ....

....

....